Getting Close to Others 5 Steps: How to Develop Intimate Relationships and Still Be True to Yourself

Getting Close to Others
5 Steps: How to Develop
Intimate Relationships and
Still Be True to Yourself

THE RELATIONSHIP FORMULA WORKBOOK SERIES

Jill P. Weber, PhD

ISBN: 1548734187
ISBN 13: 9781548734183
Library of Congress Control Number: 2017910855
CreateSpace Independent Publishing Platform
North Charleston, South Carolina

About the Author

Jill P. Weber, PhD, is a clinical psychologist in private practice in Washington, DC. She is the author of *Having Sex, Wanting Intimacy: Why Women Settle for One-Sided Relationships*. She writes a relationship and self-esteem blog for *Psychology Today*. Her writing has appeared in the *Huffington Post* as well as in *Healthy Living Magazine* and *USA Today*, and she is a psychology contributor to various media outlets, including the *Washington Post*, *Nightline*, CNN, Discovery Channel, and the Associated Press.

The Relationship Formula Workbook Series

1. *Breaking Up and Divorce 5 Steps: How to Heal and Be Comfortable Alone*
2. *Building Self-Esteem 5 Steps: How to Feel "Good Enough" about Yourself*
3. *Toxic Love 5 Steps: How to Identify Toxic-Love Patterns and Find Fulfilling Attachments*
4. *Getting Close to Others 5 Steps: How to Develop Intimate Relationships and Still Be True to Yourself*

Contents

Preface

Most people who fear intimacy want intimacy. This quandary makes them feel unhappy and hopeless. Although these individuals may have relationships, the other people in their lives see them as aloof and guarded, and interpret this quality as a form of rejection, and respond in kind. And when this happens, the ones who fear intimacy blame and criticize themselves because they are usually well aware that they go through life reflexively shutting out others.

Those living with these contradictory feelings are uncomfortable with the prospect of being fully known. This leads them to criticize, distract, and conceal to avoid revealing their true selves. They may be in close physical proximity to others, but they live in a bubble of emotional solitude. People who struggle with intimacy often believe that close relationships will bring either rejection or its opposite, total engulfment. The belief that you cannot be your own person in a relationship or that you cannot reliably depend on another person to have your needs met can be deeply disturbing.

People I work with who have had trouble getting outside of this bubble usually hold a rigid belief that human beings either have an ability to get close to others or they do not. They see intimacy as fixed and out of their control. Please hear me on this: intimacy is not an innate gift—it is a skill to be cultivated. People who have never before experienced real closeness can actually do so. I have seen this happen many times.

With practice, intimacy will happen for you. And it can be powerfully impactful. As I tell my clients, it only takes one person to change your intimacy path forever. The first time you feel that another being is close to you and knows you will entirely alter your future relationship trajectory. You will no longer settle for being half known, or for one-sided relationships, or for sublimating your needs in favor of putting all of your energy into taking care of the needs of another.

Intimacy and closeness consist of back-and-forth conversations, physical exchanges, and time spent together. As the process unfolds, communication is honest—expressions of sentiments can be revisited and revised. The key is direct conversation. For example: "Oh, I realized when we were talking I didn't mention X," or "I feel I said too much last night, and now wish I had held back a bit," or "I'd love to see you today," or "I'd love to see you today and at the same time I'm worried we are moving too fast," or "I realized yesterday when I pulled away I seemed angry with you, but actually I was scared," or "I want to tell you more about myself but I'm afraid you won't like what you hear," or "Some of the things you told me about yourself made me nervous, can we talk about it again."

Getting close to others is about being your real self, celebrating the real selves of others in your life, and setting down your own limits in your relationships while also accepting the limits of others.

Picture a boat safely tied to a dock. At times the boat will drift away from the dock, and the lines that hold it will be taut. At other times the boat will hover close, and the lines will be slack. Emotional closeness doesn't mean there isn't room to move. The sturdy lines of an intimate connection keep two people close and allow them to weather emotional fluctuations.

There are as many ways to get close to someone and to be known as there are variances in human personalities. As you read and complete the exercises in this workbook, you will learn the specifics of what you need to draw from within yourself and from others to feel safely close to another being.

Perhaps you, like many others, are afraid to take this step in attempting to forge the deeply connected types of relationships you desire. For you, beginning to work on growing close to others feels like diving into cold, cold water. Take the work one step at time, put a toe in here and there, and eventually you will find warmth.

Out of the dark cup
Your voice broke like a flower.
It trembled, swaying on its taut stem.
The caress in its touch
Made my eyes close.

From "The Telephone," by Florence Ripley Mastin

Special note: Keep a notebook handy so you can write down your answers to the exercises in this workbook. Review the notebook from time to time to remind yourself of what you are learning about yourself as you grow through this program. The more you review the material and practice, the more the material will serve you.

STEP 1

Get to Know Yourself

Much of my work as a clinical psychologist is centered on helping people learn ways to get close to others safely. Those struggling with intimacy frame their fear of closeness in different ways:

"I'm terrified of being known."

"I want to be known, but I don't know how to let people in."

"No one will love me if they actually get to know me."

"I have to hide my true self to be loved."

"I have been hiding for so long I don't know how to let people in."

"I act like a dick when I feel close to someone."

"I become very needy when I know I'm getting closer to someone."

"I'm around people all the time, but I feel so alone."

"When I feel close, I pull away."

"When I feel like someone is really trying to get to know me, I become awkward and withdraw."

"I prefer to talk about others rather than myself."

"I feel empty."

"When I'm sad, I put on a happy face."

"I fantasize that someone will read my mind and know me and love me."

"The moment I realize I'm close to someone is precisely the moment I turn on them."

It is often easier for a person to focus on what they are not getting from others than it is to focus on what they are not getting from themselves. With this in mind, consider that fear of intimacy often springs from a lack of self-knowledge and self-acceptance. There are remedies for this.

Self-knowledge means you understand what makes you tick, what makes you happy, what brings you pleasure or triggers rage. Self-acceptance means that you do not beat yourself up with self-criticism for who you are. You may wish to change and find ways to grow as a human, but this can be done with an abundance of warmth and understanding when done by means of self-acceptance.

If you tell yourself, "You're impossible; you're never going to be good enough," or "No one will ever love me," then you are blocking your own ability to get close to another person. Talk to yourself with kindness and you will become self-assured. It is self-assurance that allows people to grow, to take risks, and to accept challenges.

If you are constantly down on yourself for what you don't have or will never be, then you lack a stable platform on which to grow. And when this is the case, self-loathing and fear turn new experiences and challenges into impossible hurdles. Keep in mind that you cannot be emotionally intimate with others if you are hostile with yourself. This involves learning how to be alone contentedly as well as how to understand and accept your emotional self. You can't skip this step—if you can't accept and tolerate your own self, then why would anyone else accept it?

Problem: "I hate being alone."
Cure: Learn to depend on yourself.

To know yourself and to love yourself, you have to feel as if you can depend on YOU to weather life's adversity. This means that you believe you can manage what comes your way without having to be dependent on a rescuer and without seeing yourself as a mostly helpless victim. This is not as easy a task as many think. Some people assume they have achieved emotional self-sufficiency when in reality they have not. For example, if a parent figure is always there to bail you out, then you will not evaluate romantic partners from a perspective that is all your own. If you continue to depend upon an ex-spouse, ex-girlfriend, or ex-boyfriend to meet your emotional needs, then you have not learned to take emotional care of yourself. It may also mean that when you date someone new, you go in with awkward baggage because you are still emotionally dependent upon an old flame.

As much as possible, little by little, work to be independent of your parents or past romantic relationships. Work to become comfortable making your own decisions. Excessively asking for others' opinions, reassurance, or guidance or allowing them to control your life means you are not living for yourself. And if you allow others to continually do the heavy lifting for you, then you will not be a whole person when the right match presents itself.

Entering into a romantic relationship believing that someone is going to take care of you in the way your parents or ex-partners did can turn a healthy match into a toxic one. To be prepared to let a new love into your life, you have to be in control of your life, as well as being aware of your goals, needs, and emotions.

Exercise: Be Alone

Work to be self-sufficient and content alone. This is the path to self-confidence. Travel this way and you will no longer be desperate to partner up. You will welcome new relationships, but without the agitation of someone frightened by the prospect of being, even briefly, alone. Frenetic socializing will give way to a naturally reinforcing balance between social and solitary existence.

Take on the following behaviors with regularity to help yourself become comfortable interweaving your solitary and social selves.

- *Develop a tolerance for yourself, on your own, without others around.* Perhaps you go from one social event to the next, work long hours, and constantly have activities to fill your spare time. When you do have a moment alone, you feel uncomfortable and immediately find ways to busy yourself. Ask yourself: What are you avoiding by being so busy? Are you afraid of quiet time? What is the hardest part for you about being alone? Allow your emotions to come in and be felt. Accept those feelings. See if you can learn something new about yourself simply by being quiet and feeling whatever may come to mind when you are alone. Actively show yourself that you can deal with the discomfort that being alone brings. Observe how tolerating and labeling the uneasiness allows it to fade.

- *Meditate for ten minutes a day.* Learn to be contentedly alone through meditating each day for ten minutes. Your only goal is to sit somewhere quietly and comfortably while you bring your full awareness to your breath. Each time you become aware of your thoughts drifting, gently pull your attention back to your breath. Notice your chest rising and falling or any sounds you hear around you. Work over and over again to bring your attention back to your breathing and to the sensations in your body. You are not making a mistake when your thoughts drift away; that is natural. But what helps the brain to restore is the process of bringing your attention back again and again to your breath.

- **Imagine what you want:** If you don't make time for yourself to thoughtfully consider what you want, what you want might never come. Spend one half hour a week sitting quietly and imagining what you wish for yourself. Picture your life going the way you want it to go—including your work, relationships, finances, and health. Bring your full attention to the picture as you visualize exactly what you want to feel inside and what you want to be doing on the outside. Imagine obstacles and challenges, but find ways around these challenges in your visualization. Use this imaginary problem solving to limit the time spent feeling badly about yourself when something does not work out. Instead, when you hit a setback, sit quietly and imagine a more effective/helpful reaction to the same event.

- **Consider Your Thinking Self.** You no longer need to be a lady or gentleman, waiting for Mr. or Mrs. Right to come along and make you feel good. You have the power to make yourself feel good. Search for new aspects of your identity that have yet to be explored and that are separate from your relationships with others. Whenever a relationship is going less than smoothly, you can turn to your work or other interests for needed validation and meaning. Allow yourself to consider what it is that may satisfy your thinking self. Examples of such pursuits could include taking on new professional endeavors, pursuing artistic interests, developing one's spirituality, taking an interest in politics, pursuing intellectual interests, taking a leadership position, volunteering, or going back to school. You don't need to be the best at or perfect at your pursuit. You just need to feel intellectually stimulated by, excited by, or curious about the work. This activity is intended for you, not for your appearance to others.

- **Build Healthy Routines of Functioning.** This means considering developing a deliberate schedule for your week. Build time into this schedule for meditating, being quietly and peacefully alone, as well as for two or three interactive activities, such as social events, group meetings, book clubs, hobbies, or dinner with a friend. In addition, schedule time each week for grocery shopping, chores around your home, errands, gym or yoga time, and managing your bills or general paperwork. Sticking to a regular routine that you keep more days than not is probably the single best way for healthy people to stay grounded and connected to themselves. This routine will give you a sturdy support structure.

- *Foster Healthy Friendships.* Attach yourself to healthy people. People who make you feel worse, judged, or criticized on a continual basis are detrimental to the work you are doing for yourself. Instead, connect with people with whom you can be authentic—that is, free of pretending or false fronts. These are people who will not overwhelm or dismiss you. Also pick people who you like to listen to and for whom you have empathy or a deeper connection. Much like developing a romantic attachment, cultivating healthy and deep friendship takes effort. It's important to be vulnerable and to let people in, but do choose friends carefully and take notice when you are mistreated. If you feel overly controlled or dismissed, put your experience into words and talk to them about it. If they cannot accept where you are, what you need, or your boundaries, consider that the friendship may not be a healthy one.

Learning to be alone and to make your own decisions is a process. Start the process now. Each step you take toward accepting that you can depend on yourself will bring you new confidence and security.

Problem: "I feel awkward in new relationships."
Cure: Understand yourself emotionally.
If you don't feel close to yourself, you cannot develop healthy close relationships with others. Instead, you will rely on self-defeating shortcuts—hastened sex, one-sided dependency, alcohol—and you will have a high tolerance for destructive relationships. Is beating your head against a wall by reenacting self-defeating patterns better than committing to doing the hard work of embracing your authentic self?

Take the case of Natalie. As a college freshman, Natalie often thought she was falling behind in everything. When she entered social groups, she felt she was an outsider and never part of a welcoming clique or social support system that she could depend upon. Alone in her dorm room, she struggled with a sense of empti-ness and was uncertain about how to spend her time. She struggled with classes, unsure about which direction to take her studies. She was constantly in search of distraction to take her away from herself. She used socializing, partying, and guys as a way to feel more alive and more valuable than she felt on a day-to-day basis. When she was out, she flirted with men and used sex and hooking up as a way to get close. She had a fantasy that a hookup would eventually lead to something special that would take her away from her chronic uneasiness and discontent. Yet every time she hooked up, she felt worse and more alone than ever. She was upset and depleted with no real understanding of why.

The cycle of using sex to achieve more emotional closeness and self-validation is something I term "sextimacy." I detail what sextimacy is in my book, *Having Sex, Wanting Intimacy*. If you use relationships, sex, or risky activities to avoid yourself, I encourage you to hit the pause button. Step back and confront all you have been avoiding. Consider that the one person you cannot get rid of is yourself. With that in mind, the importance of understanding yourself emotionally is crucial to your happiness and success in life.

Understanding Your Emotional Self

Perhaps you know when you are upset or happy, but start taking a nuanced look at the mild fluctuations in your feelings that occur on a day-to-day basis. Small emotional fluctuations accumulate, eventually leading to "bad" or "good" moods. The more you know what you are feeling *when you are feeling it* and why, the more control you will have over your ability to make yourself feel better. Also, you need to have a nuanced understanding of your emotions so you can eventually com-municate them more effectively to your romantic partners (step 5).

You can't be close to yourself if you don't accept every aspect of your ex-perience. Acknowledging and validating all of your emotions, not just the posi-tive ones, brings security. Knowing that you know yourself, in this intimate way, will help you to feel less dependent. Also, the more you understand your own emotions, the easier it is to read and understand the emotions and motives of others.

Make room for each emotion with warm acceptance, so that you can deal with whatever comes up. Just as you would take care of a child or loved one who is emotionally upset, generously provide the wounded one—that's you—with nur-turance, not aggravation.

There are four components in the development of healthy emotional awareness: noticing how your body is changing in reaction to emotional stimuli; finding the label that best describes what you are feeling; accepting the emotion you are experiencing; and noticing the type of attention you are giving the emotion.

▪ *Notice the Physical*

For every feeling we have, there is a corresponding bodily sensation and physi-cal urge to do something in response. As a function of brain processes, emotions initiate changes in blood pressure, heart rate, muscle tension, and in the diges-tive tract. We have become so accustomed to our body's responses to emotion that we often do not notice these changes. By developing physical awareness, you will increase your control of your reactions. Tune in, from the inside out, to the changes occurring in your body.

The experience of anger, for example, usually involves a tensing of the muscles and an urge to aggress against someone or something. One client I worked with discovered her jaw became tight when she was angry. As she tuned into this feel-ing, she became aware of her anger long before it got out of control and became destructive. Similarly, sadness is often accompanied by heaviness in the heart and a lethargic feeling. Anxiety and fear may involve an increase in heart rate or ten-sion in the gut, while pleasure often manifests itself in a lack of muscle tension and a restful sensation.

▪ *Identify What You Are Feeling*

The next essential component for healthy emotional attunement is your ability to choose the label that best describes what you are feeling. Many people are able to do this easily, but for those who suppress their emotions, differentiating their feel-ings requires effort. Noticing sensations in your body will help you to distinguish and separate your feelings. This will let you more distinctly recognize when you are angry, sad, anxious, or happy, as well as appreciating the finer nuances that make feelings unique. When you're stuck, it can be helpful to ask yourself questions: What is my body trying to communicate to me about how I feel in this situation?

What area of my body is the most noticeable to me at this moment? What is it signaling?

If you are keyed up and tense, you are probably worried and anxious. If your muscles feel relaxed, you may be feeling pleasure. Examine how you feel physically and then ask yourself this question: Is this a signal of fear, sadness, hurt, or anger? As you find the label that most aptly applies to what you are feeling, you will know it: identifying the feeling should bring some relief.

▪ *Accept What You Are Feeling*

Once you have a label that aptly describes your physical experience, accept that feeling. You are not trying to replay the facts of the situation. You are not trying to justify or even to talk yourself out of what you are feeling. You have the feeling, and you have labeled it. It is real. Denying it would mean you are unable to know yourself on an authentic level. Even if you push the feelings away, they still exist and will probably come out indirectly. You may seem, suddenly and dramatically, to be acting inappropriately to others in your life when you indirectly express feelings that you are denying to yourself.

The process of accepting your emotions should not involve conjuring empathy for the other person in the situation. Just stick with what *you* are feeling. Tell yourself that it is perfectly okay to experience whatever you are experiencing. Alternatively, if you say to yourself, "I don't want this, I shouldn't feel this," or "He had a busy week, I should be more sensitive to his needs," then you are invalidating yourself.

For example, if you felt a hunger pain, would you tell yourself "I am not hungry, I have no reason to feel hungry, there must something wrong with me"? I hope not. It is important to believe what your body and mind are telling you and to remember that your experience of your life is valid. If you say, "Of course I'm sad, I miss my boyfriend and I like spending time with him," you are validating yourself. If you are angry, validate this feeling; you can love someone and simultaneously be angry with them. Acknowledging anger in your own mind will not destroy a relationship.

▪ *Give Kind Attention to What You Are Feeling.*

It is of utmost importance to notice the type of attention you are giving to what you are feeling. Consider whether or not you are self-critical, and, if you are self-critical, develop open-minded labels for what you are feeling as well as a kind, internal tone. Notice when you are using disapproving terms to describe your experience, such as "It is bad to feel this...I am weak for feeling sad...Why do I always feel sorry for myself." Statements like these muddy the water and make it impossible for you to assess your circumstances rationally.

The goal is to know what you feel without losing your self-esteem in the process. Overwhelming yourself with harsh criticism prevents you from looking at specific emotions that can be identified and eventually put into perspective. As opposed to questioning what you are feeling, simply label whatever you notice—stomach feels tense, head burns, tears fall, heart pounding, mind restless. Attunement requires back-and-forth, conscious attention to what is occurring in your body, followed up by efforts to label the feelings. *Examine your emotions without becoming engulfed by them.*

Exercise: Feelings Table

If you have difficulty knowing what you are feeling in the moment, use this chart as an aid in labeling what it is that you are *really* feeling. Doing this will help you pay attention to the important data your emotions are giving you about yourself and the people in your life.

Emotions	Physical/Bodily Sensations	Labels to Describe Your Experience	Action Urges	Evolutionary Significance
Love	Calm body, relaxed muscles, sense of internal peace and well-being	Sense of comfort, safety, comfort with another, passion, sexual longing	Desire to be with the person, to bond with the other, to make sure the other is okay	Love bonds couples, children, families, and tribes together. It is the glue that connects people.
Pleasure	Accompanied by the brain releasing "feel-good hormones," so you may feel increased energy, lack of physical pain; body is excited	Delight, joy, vivaciousness, contentment, mastery, feeling lost in the moment, not thinking about the future or the past	Urge to smile, laugh, talk more with others, and reveal more about yourself	Pleasure is tonic for negative emotions and motivates us to do certain things so that we may experience even more pleasure.
Anger	Body feels tense, jaw clenches, and muscles tighten; increased body temperature and a feeling of pressure behind the eyes	Feeling unfairly treated or disrespected by others or the world as a whole, outrage, rage; feeling the self is not valued	Urge to aggress or harm another, urge to yell at someone or throw something	Anger cues the body to self-protect through physical force, self-assertion, or boundary-setting.

Emotions	Physical/Bodily Sensations	Labels to Describe Your Experience	Action Urges	Evolutionary Significance
Sadness	The body wants to remain still; feeling of lethargy and a lack of energy; possibly hard to get your body to move	Loss, grief, hopelessness, rejection; feeling defeated or unwanted by others; feeling bad about the self	Urge to cry or to sit still or in one place, lack of motivation, urge to ruminate about what you did to cause the loss	Sadness is protective in that it allows the self to sit in place while grief and problem-solving can occur.
Anxiety	Stress hormones triggered by brain, which leads to muscle tension, restlessness, increased heartbeat, sweating, shortness of breath, stomachache	Being worried or fearful, feeling threatened by something in the environment or within a relationship (fear of losing a relationship), being in high-alert, vigilant, survival mode	Urge to replay events in one's mind, predict future events and desire to take control of the threat; urge to flee or busy the self	Anxiety triggers adrenaline so that the body goes into high alert. You become primed for action and protection.
Guilt	Body feels sick, stomach and muscles hurt; feels as if you can't be physically at ease	Feeling like a "bad" person, feeling destructive, feeling you should be punished	Urge to make amends and to be a "better" person, urge to berate the self	Guilt keeps people in accordance with societal laws and norms designed for protecting people.

Emotions	Physical/Bodily Sensations	Labels to Describe Your Experience	Action Urges	Evolutionary Significance
Shame	Burning sensation on the face, cheeks flushing, stomach sinking	Embarrassment, humiliation, exposure as a fraud; fearing that a flaw will be revealed to another or to the public	Urge to flee or leave the situation, urge to become invisible and hide the self from others	Shame signifies social status in a group, keeping people in accordance with group expectations.

Exercise: Use the Emotional Spreadsheet.

Force yourself to deliberately reflect on what you are feeling and what you may be burying. Once a day, sit down and spend ten to fifteen minutes alone attending to your emotional world. Sit back and allow whatever you are feeling to be present while labeling the following:

- What is the emotion you are feeling?
- What are the physical sensations that accompany the emotion?
- What are the thoughts associated with the emotion?
- What judgments are you making about your emotion?
- What memories are associated with the way you are feeling in this moment?
- What self-soothing action can you do (take a walk, bike ride, yoga, call a friend, massage, journal, go somewhere)?
- What self-soothing thought can you call to mind that brings you some comfort? (Examples include "This feeling can be here as long as it needs to be," "I am going to be okay," "Feelings are like the weather, they change," or "This feeling will pass.")

Start reflecting on your emotions in the manner described above. Once an emotion passes, another will come along. Do the exercise again for that new emotion. Engaging even your most intense emotions in this way will eventually become a constructive habit that enables you to be meaningfully connected with yourself.

STEP 2

Stop Faking It

Loneliness is inevitable when a person's default mode is to pretend to be something he or she is not. You may be on a date or surrounded by people you are interested in, and yet you cannot let go and allow yourself to be fully present and spontaneous. You leave social interactions feeling empty and left out. You beat yourself up wishing you were a better, stronger, sexier, more outgoing person. The reality of your problem is that you fail to present yourself as you actually are. People catch this vibe, and they keep their distance as a result.

When a person is uncomfortable with himself or herself, it is not surprising if the person strains to camouflage their personality. The person may have done this for so long that awareness for what he or she is doing has diminished. The facade or show has become automatic.

There is a way for a person to stop this cycle of high expectations for closeness followed by a letdown when it does not arrive. It means ending the pretending: the obscuring of appearances, preferences, feelings, and drives. Anyone can do this, but the first crucial step is for you to be authentic with yourself. Once that hurdle is crossed, authenticity with others can follow.

Problem: "I don't know why I act the way I do."
Cure: Be real within yourself.

If you struggle with self-acceptance, then you likely have a deeply rooted belief that you need to be perfect to keep others interested in you. As a result, you may put a tight lid on yourself around others or on dates.

Perhaps whatever you communicate is well thought out so you don't risk showing anyone a chink in your armor. Or you may keep conversation superficial or gossip about others to prevent anyone from looking too deeply at you. Maybe you focus excessively on other people, never revealing much at all about yourself. Some use jewelry, makeup, and plastic surgery to mask and distract. Those who fit this profile depend on bravado and brag about their accomplishments or children to keep others at bay.

It is important to keep in mind that if this is the way you present yourself then the people you encounter probably won't make an effort to understand the deeper roots of your behavior. Instead, they will perceive you as unrelatable, someone with whom they can't really connect.

Self-Assessment: What do you do to hide the real you? Camouflaging can take many forms. Do you rely on any of the behaviors below to camouflage and distract others from seeing the real you?

- Are you a chameleon? Do you change your personality and preferences depending on those you are around at the time?

- Do you act differently with men than you do with women?

- Do you act differently with women than you do with men?

- Do you engage others mainly with surface conversation and/or gossip?

- If someone starts a more serious conversation with you, do you do things to provide distraction or avoid the conversation?

- Do you focus obsessively on your external appearance?

- Do you habitually use clothes, plastic surgery, jewelry, or handbags to distract people and dress up the real you?

- Do you focus excessively on others, getting them to open up but sharing little of your feelings, opinions, or experiences?

- Are you overly meddlesome, always telling people what to do or giving gratuitous advice?

- Do you gravitate mainly toward larger groups and shy away from one-on-one interactions?

- When you are social, do you prefer to have a large group and lots of distractions?

- Do you show off or brag about your work, material possessions, or accomplishments, so that others won't see the deeper you?

What are you afraid others will see?

Remember: when you hide your deeper self from others, you eliminate all opportunities for closeness and meaningful emotional connections. Take a few moments to consider what is at the root of your need to camouflage the real you. What are you afraid others will see about you that will cause them to reject you or become disinterested? In your mind, what is the worst aspect of your personality? Consider the list below as you assess what brings you the most shame.

Self-Assessment: What are you afraid others will discover about you?

Your real desire for a relationship
Your neurosis
Your past failures at love
Your lack of serious relationships
Your family issues
Your loner status
Your lack of income
Your workaholic nature
Your addiction
Your sadness

Your inner dork
Your inner nerd
Your ego
Your dependency on others
Your self-esteem issues
Your past achievement/work failures
Your lack of intelligence
Your lack of sexual experience
Your abundance of sexual experience
Your past emotional or physical trauma(s)
Your unlovability
Your passivity
Your underachieving nature
Your perfectionistic nature
Your lethargy
Your hyperactivity
Your inability to let people in

Be open to other examples that come to mind as you read the above list and write down in your notebook the issues that seem to resonate for you. Consider reading self-help books on your issue(s) or joining a support group. Instead of being concerned about what others will think if they find out about you, start thinking from your own perspective. If the issue feels very big and hard to understand, or if you have never felt any relief from it over a considerable period of time, consider beginning psychotherapy. Working with a therapist on a weekly basis will accelerate self-understanding and your ability to communicate your struggle.

The more you know and accept yourself, they more likely you are to attract healthy partners who value the real you.

Problem: "I want others to like me so much that I don't even know what I like anymore."
Cure: Cultivate *your* perspective and then communicate it.

A surefire, easy way to avoid risking rejection is to change your personality, preferences, and behaviors based on the people around you. Those adopting this tactic risk losing a grip on what their preferences actually are. And figuring out what those preferences are may become so daunting that it starts to seem easier to just go with the flow set by others. As a result, the people in your life learn to expect you to go along to get along. In these circumstances, we suppress preferences in fear of rejection if they're expressed.

Cognitive dissonance is a psychology concept describing what happens when a person's thoughts or feelings conflict with the way he or she acts and behaves. One example might be telling your new date that you would love to attend a heavy metal concert with him, although you know you are not a fan of this kind of music. Behaving in ways that don't actually match your internal sense of self creates anxiety and only moves you further away from being comfortable and at ease with others.

Start noticing if you find yourself agreeing to things with the knowledge that you don't really like them or want to do them. As soon as you recognize that you are engaging in cognitive dissonance, stop that specific behavior. Simply tell those around you that you changed your mind or that you thought about it and now have a better sense of what you want.

The more a person's inner and outer selves match, the easier it is to get close to others.

Self-Assessment: Develop awareness for your overall preferences. If you don't take time to consider what you like and don't like, and what you want and don't want, then it is all too easy to be swept up in the preferences and desires of others. Consider the following questions as you become more in tune with your perspective.

- What is your favorite food?

- Do you like a certain kind of music, are your tastes eclectic, or is music not your thing?

- Are you interested in certain types of movies, books, or other media?

- Do you want a serious relationship?

- Are you close to your family?

- Do you like constant activity, more solitary time, or a combination of both?

- Do you like romantic or active dates?

- Are you emotional or more stoic?

- Are you an emotional nurturer?

- Do completion of tasks and making achievements bring you good feelings about yourself?

- Does connecting with others bring you good feelings about yourself?

- What activities bring you joy?

- What types of personalities (or actual people you know) make you more at ease with yourself?

- What is your idea of the perfect night out? Perfect night in?

- What do you do when you are alone?

- What do you enjoy most about your family?

- What is the hardest part about your family?

- Do you want children?

- If you already have children, do you want the people you date to get to know your children and participate in their care?

- If you already have children, what do you need to see in or feel about a new love interest to become comfortable introducing that person to your children?

- How do you motivate yourself to do what you need to do?

- What do you think happens when we die?

- Do you have a political leaning, or do you not follow politics?

- What brings you pleasure?

- What are your quirks?

- What are your pet peeves?

The more you reflect on these items, and any of your idiosyncratic preferences, the easier it will be to know what you want and to effectively communicate your preferences when you're around others. There are no right or wrong answers, the point is to be honest about what you like and do not like. Get accustomed to pausing and checking in with yourself about how you truly feel about whatever you are encountering.

Exercise: Be real about your relationship preferences.

Knowing what you want romantically and where you have gone wrong in the past is important when you are trying to get close to others. So often when dating people tell others "I don't want a *real* relationship," when in fact they actually truly do want a real relationship. If you cannot say what you want, what you want will never come. Also, knowing your past romantic mistakes will prevent you from repeating them.

- *Reflect on what your romantic desire is, truly.* Do you want commitment? Eventually marriage? What do you need from a potential partner to be happy, to feel well cared for and loved? Do you have a fantasy about what you would like, even if you do not believe you can get it? Write down in your notebook, just for yourself, what your innermost self wants and desires. Stop telling yourself you won't get it; just let it be present and consciously focus on it.

- *Understand your history with love.* Be real with yourself about your role in past relationships and how you may have prevented yourself from getting more of what you want from others. Below are a few common ways people self-sabotage in romance. Do you tend toward any of these?

"I can do it all." Believing you can and should do it all—emotionally, financially, physically, socially—both for yourself but also for your partner sets you up for trouble. If you don't believe you can rely on others, ask for help, or be vulnerable at times, then you are probably taking on more than is healthy. You may have suppressed your own feelings so thoroughly that you do not realize how frazzled this impossible load has made you. Find other ways to connect with your partners besides always doing for them and managing their lives. Being self-reliant when necessary is a strength; being compulsively self-reliant is a curse.

"I can't do it myself." The opposite of the "I can do it all" belief is believing you cannot do anything without another warm body present to guide you, stand by your side, and do things for you. Resentment builds when a partner becomes an emotional caregiver. If your whole wellbeing rests on someone else, then you will eventually grow to feel desperate and fearful at the thought of losing them. When you think you cannot do something on your own—including work, social outings, managing difficult emotions, or taking a risk—do it in spite of yourself! Show your partner or future partners that you are a living, breathing, effective human being, all on your own. Then, they can enjoy you without the burden of feeling emotionally responsible for you.

"I'm afraid to get what I want." I see it so often in my psychotherapy practice: a person wanting nothing more than to attach to a healthy partner for a long-term relationship. Yet once the match presents itself, panic sets in. The person may list Seinfeld-like quirks such as "When he chews his food he hums." But once we get a little below the surface, invariably we find a fear of failure in the person making the list. "What if I can't provide for her financially?" "What if I can't be available in the way he needs?" "What if he hates my family?" "What if I can't please her?" The list goes on. Some fear is inevitable when one person begins to feel close with another and warms to the idea that a meaningful match may be possible. It is much easier to want something you cannot have. Once you know you can have it, a little fear is kindled. A fear that you will not be able to give the situation what it needs to grow. Talk yourself off this ledge. Instead of going internal, discuss your fears. There is nothing more comforting than sharing our concerns with others and having them met with love and understanding.

"I'm afraid I will be found out." If you are in a healthy union your partner will inevitably find out about your flaws. The reality is that happy relationships, romantic or not, take accountability. When those closest to you see your flaws and weaknesses, they are getting to know you fully. Explain yourself and how you got this way. Take responsibility when you hurt others or let them down. Being less than perfect doesn't mean you are a miserable failure; it means you are a real, living human being others can connect with. The problems I see come when couples hold themselves to impossible standards so that each puts on a show for the other or for the public. Acting out a façade keeps people at a distance and makes for awkward and inhibited social and physical interactions.

"I'll have to change." Love is fun—flirty texts during the day, spontaneous meet ups during the workweek, and sleepovers on the weekend. Once the newness fades, though, you may find yourself overwhelmed at the idea of eventually living with someone or having to adjust your routine, future goals, and day-to-day habits to accommodate someone else. Yet change is inevitable. What type of life would you have if you merely did the same thing for the next forty years? Don't deny the impact of your new situation, but do find a way to talk with your partner about changes that are more challenging for you. See if you can problem solve together about ways to accommodate each other, ensuring that the changes you do make are not made too soon or are not overly abrupt.

Do not obfuscate about what you need from others to be happy and about what you need to develop to be a good partner to your future love interest.

Exercise: Practice presenting your real self to others.

You hear it so often when it comes to dating, and I can remember my own mom saying it: "Just be yourself and it will go fine." If only it were that easy! On second thought, maybe it could be?

Hopefully, the exercises in this workbook thus far are causing you to reflect more deeply on who you are and what you want. Now, work very hard to share this perspective with others in your life. You can do this through new dates, family members, friends, or acquaintances. Practice only saying and doing what actually matches the way you feel and what you believe. Develop awareness of times when you are adopting the perspective of someone else, and work to keep your own perspective alive by talking about your viewpoint and discussing it openly.

If you are dreading seeing a particular person or find you have to gear up before meeting him or her, then consider that you may not be your authentic self with that person. If you don't feel warm and at ease after interacting with a person, reflect on these questions: Is this someone with whom you could be more like yourself? What is stopping you? Is the person self-centered and unable to listen and be open to you?

Practice clearly stating what you are like as a person and as a partner with trusted others, and what your strengths and weaknesses are in loving others. There will come a time when you will need to communicate this to the new people you date and, similarly, you will want to date those who can do the same.

Bringing a halt to inauthenticity means the following: if you feel uncomfortable, "yucky," tense, or anxious, then consider pausing before you overcompensate by engaging in inauthentic communication.

Communicating with Boundaries

Becoming close and intimate with others requires a series of conversations and interactions over time, each of which encourages closeness. You should not dive in immediately. Instead, allow the process to unfold naturally. Talk about yourself, of course, but start with the least threatening aspects of your inner self and then move deeper over time.

Even at the beginning of new relationships, *never ever say anything false about yourself or your preferences.* If you find you have done so inadvertently, tell the person you are getting close to that you misspoke and correct the information, so that you are providing an accurate reflection of who you are. Otherwise, what you are building together isn't real and will not bring you peace and comfort.

Exercise: Tell three people about yourself.

This week, pick three people with whom you can confide. If you have never done so previously, tell them you are working on being a more open person and that you hope they will listen with a warm ear. Share with them the patterns you have been working to break, your newfound preferences, or your new goals for your future relationships. Let these people know the ways in which you are growing. You do not have to share every detail, and if others ask questions you are not ready to answer, simply say, "I think that's all I can say about it at this point, I'm still figuring it out. Thank you for listening." Regularly sharing this side of yourself with a few trusted friends will help you to become more at ease with presenting your authentic self to others.

STEP 3

Explore Your Sexual Self

Connecting with yourself emotionally and knowing your preferences is similar to connecting with yourself with regard to sex. And as always, the more comfortable a person is with himself or herself, the less likely that person is to resort to self-defeating behavior that pushes others away. Consider the examples below of James and Suzanna, and how being disconnected from their sexual selves thwarts emotional intimacy in their romantic relationships.

James loved his wife and would do anything for her. Nonetheless, there was a tremendous amount of tension in his marriage. James's wife was suspicious of his relationships with other women. Every now and again she would discover flirty texts or evidence of his interactions with past flames on social media. She never felt as if she had his full attention, and when they were out, she routinely observed him staring at other women.

James found that whenever he was sexual with his wife, he was preoccupied by anxious thoughts: "Will she like that...what does she like...will she think I'm a freak if I try that...am I pleasing her...is she enjoying this or just putting up with it...if I act out my sexual fantasy, is she going to think I'm perverted?" These worries caused him to be extremely self-conscious. He found that these thoughts were not present when he had had commitment-free sex with other women. In these no-strings relationships, he was more able to be himself sexually. He believed this was because he did not worry about what his partner thought or how they were experiencing him.

Over time, he turned increasingly to online pornography, where he could be anonymous, without concern about how he was coming across to his real-life partner. These behaviors were devastating to his wife, who felt profoundly unloved and undesired. In therapy, James described splitting sex from love.

Suzanna grew up shy and introverted. Throughout her childhood, her family moved every year for professional reasons. She was always the new girl in school and felt excluded and alone in this role. She learned by eighth grade that making herself sexually available to her teenage, male counterparts gave her a degree of acceptance. She recalled instances where she might feel down at not being invited to a classmate's party and then feel thrilled when, out of the blue, a guy would call her for a late-evening rendezvous.

There were several insidious side effects to this mode of achieving peer acceptance. For one, the feeling of being liked wore off quickly, which left Suzanna perpetually in search of her next quick fix. In between hook-ups, Suzanna felt empty and ashamed. She had trouble feeling good about what she "had to do" to keep men in her life. Finally, as Suzanna's high school years went by, so too did the opportunities to build her self-esteem and to learn the skills necessary to forge mutually fulfilling relationships with men.

By the time she entered college, she felt self-conscious and awkward when she found herself one-on-one with a man in a context that did not involve sexual contact. Suzanna would become so anxious that she would impulsively make the relationship sexual as soon as possible. This coping mechanism offered Suzanna a short reprieve from her anxiety, as the men involved were more than willing to accommodate. Nonetheless, she did not enjoy the sexual encounters, and once they were completed, she was left to feel even more internally defeated. She believed full acceptance and a genuine connection with a man were permanently out of her reach.

This kind of dating, quickly short-circuiting to sex, eventually spun off into a marriage. However, the hurry-up process never required her husband to actually get to know more than one dimension of her. In order for this relationship to work, she became a chameleon taking on the identity of her husband. And, after five years of marriage, Suzanna recognized that her husband did not know her because she never revealed her true self.

Because she didn't feel known or genuinely valued by her husband, Suzanna reverted to her old coping strategy and became drawn into an affair with a co-worker quite easily. The cycle from her past repeated itself; she felt a temporary self-esteem surge, followed by prolonged feelings of guilt and shame, which she managed with negative self-appraisals: "I am an awful person...I am a horrible wife...no one will ever like me for who I am...I am weak...how could anyone want to be with me?" These painfully harsh judgments led to a depleted self, which powered an even stronger need for instant validation.

For Suzanne and for James, there is a debilitating gap between sex and intimacy. Those who face this gap in their lives can bridge it with insight and practice.

Problem: "Sex always plays out the same way for me; it's like watching a scene in a movie over and over again."
Cure: Cultivate *your* sexual narrative.

Men and women are often limited in their sexual expression by cultural stereotypes. An individual may not be conscious of the influence of these stereotypes. Nevertheless, they can become barriers to creating a fulfilling sexual and emotional experience.

For example, it is not unusual for women follow a male narrative of sex. They may derive sexual pleasure solely through awareness of their partner's desire. They only feel desirable if they are providing sexual pleasure, and they become awkward and self-conscious when receiving it. The more prone a woman is to see herself through the eyes of her partner, the harder it is for her to know her own pleasure. For a woman, sexual pleasure occurs not only through understanding her body, but also through knowing what stimulates her mind. In order to enjoy sex, it's important for her to develop a narrative that serves her mind and body.

There can be a disconnect for some men between the way they view the partners they love or believe they could love and the way they view those people they simply wish to have sex with. Some men fear that bringing their full sexual self into the picture with their committed partner will negatively overwhelm this partner. Others may be attentive to their partners' needs for a limited period of time. After the newness of the relationship wears off, they might feel it is too much effort to make sure another person is happy while also focusing on their own drives. As a result, they become less spontaneous and more inhibited with their committed partners.

These men report that, for them to enjoy sex fully, it has to be with certain "types" of people about whose judgments they don't really care. As a result, they may divide the people they meet into "marriage material" and "sex material." This is ultimately disempowering for men, because in order for them to have enjoyable sexual experiences, they must lie and hide their behavior from their committed partner. In the end, they limit how deep and meaningful their committed relationships can be and often feel bad about themselves as a result.

Exercise: Explore Your Sexual Narrative

Consider your point of view about sex: what is your narrative for how sex should proceed? Notice your judgments about yourself and others, and how these judgments may keep you from fully understanding your sexual self and from having a fulfilling sex life.

Self-Assessment: What is your sexual narrative?

- Do you feel you have to act a certain way to keep your partners happy with you?

- What is tolerable, intolerable, pleasurable, or uncomfortable in your sexual narrative?

- Write down a sexual fantasy, or if you don't have one, work to develop one now. Next, write down how your sexual experiences usually go. Is there any overlap between your fantasy and reality? If not, there should be—so ask yourself: Why not? Why are you holding back? What are you afraid will happen if you share this part of yourself with your intimate partners?

- Do you believe sex is to be enjoyed by you or is it mainly for him? Do you have a narrative that men are just "out for one thing" or are sexual predators?

- Are women who enjoy sex loose or slutty? Do you feel that if you enjoy sex with the mother of your children, that is somehow "dirty" or "bad"? Do you divide the people you meet into either sex objects or committed partners?

- If women feel sexual in their own bodes does that make them "trashy" or "slutty"?

- Can you imagine a new narrative of merging enjoyable sexual experiences with someone you are also emotionally close to? If not, what gets in the way? List what you fear will happen if you are open in all ways with one person.

- Do you see sex as something men take and women give? If so, and if you are a woman, how do you think this may inhibit your enjoyment of sex? And if you are a man, how do you think this mentality might make it hard for you to merge emotional and sexual pleasure with the same partner?

- Does your pleasure narrative stop with giving your partner pleasure? Can you imagine yourself and your partner both being pleased and connected during the sex act?

- Is it hard to feel desire for your sexual partner unless it is in a detached, souped-up, vaguely pornographic scenario? What purpose does the detachment of pornography provide for you? When you have real-life sex, are you self-conscious or anxious about what your partner thinks, so that pornography becomes the only way you can let yourself go completely? Could you imagine what blocks would need to be removed within you for you to be less inhibited with your real-life partners?

If you narrowly focus on cultural stereotypes about men and women, you forgo the opportunity to learn what you desire, and your sexual pleasure will remain elusive. Notice when you are going to the external, that is, seeing the world in terms of the way you think your partners or society view you. Instead, try to see yourself, your sexual needs and desires, separate from stereotypes. Take responsibility for enjoying your sex life by developing a new sexual narrative that includes your fantasies and preferences. The more you believe you are a sexual being and that sex is an important aspect of your identity, the easier it will be for you to develop a fulfilling and pleasurable sex life with a committed partner.

Problem: "I'm not sure I have fully connected with my sexual self."
Cure: Explore and communicate.

To fully claim your sexuality, it's important to consider your first sexual learning experiences. Just as is true for emotional development, one's ideas about sexuality are based on patterns that were imprinted early on in your development. Consider what you were told as a child about your sexual anatomy, and how you learned about the birds and the bees.

For example, girls become anxious instead of curious and explorative when they are told to not touch "down there," or that only bad girls have sex. Overemphasis on what teenage girls are wearing and implying that bad things happen to girls who dress certain ways communicates to girls that if something bad happens, it is their fault. All of these messages trap girls in a net of caution and fear that thwarts enjoyment of or connection with their sexual experiences.

Similarly, boys are frequently conditioned to equate masculinity with sexual conquest and sexual detachment. For some men, relief for this impossible equation is found in addictive pornography usage or in maintaining multiple, concurrent sexual partners. Living out pornographic sex helps these men indulge a fantasy that their power is found in the types of sexual experiences they can attain—even if only in fantasy. Of course, sadly, the reality is that men with addictions to pornography or sex are terribly detached from their partners and carry shame that they cannot better enjoy real-life sex with a real-life partner.

Escaping a pattern of disconnected sex means learning to look at your sexual self through a different lens. Consider the following questions.

Self-Assessment: What were your first experiences with sex?

- When you were growing up, what were you told about sex? What were you told about your body parts? Was shame induced about self-touch? Remember the labels you were taught, and what your parents' attitudes were toward your sexuality as well as toward sex in general.

- How did your mother and father, each as individuals, react when your body began to change in adolescence? Did they help you to better understand what was happening? Did your parents caution you that guys were out for one thing? Did they tell you "Have fun but don't get pregnant"? Or was it "Have fun, but don't get her pregnant"? Did they take excessive interest in controlling your dress and appearance? Or, in retrospect, did you need more limits or protection than they provided?

- Did your parents say nothing at all about the birds and the bees or about understanding your changing body? Did they tell you "boys will be boys" or subtly make you feel as if you weren't really a man/woman until you were sexually active? Did they offer the idea of not having sex unless you also want an emotional relationship with the same person? Or did you get the idea that relationships are hopelessly complicated and full of drama, thereby learning to separate sex from emotional connection?

- Did your parents, media, or pornography directly or indirectly communicate to you that women who are sexual are somehow trashy or slutty?

- Did your parents appear to have any kind of real closeness between them? Or did you get the idea that commitment and passion cannot coexist?

- Your sexual blueprint is developed through your first sexual experiences with romantic partners and then by each subsequent sexual experience over time. This is a good reason to choose your partners thoughtfully. Review your first sexual experiences and consider what themes emerge.

- Was your sexuality treated with respect in your family and, likewise, do you pick partners who treat you with respect? Or when you were young, were you told little about your developing sexuality, except by means of criticism or caution, and likewise now pick partners who make you feel guarded and judged? Were you taught to respect your sexual partners, to treat them as full beings, or were you told close to nothing about how to merge sex and emotional connection?

Challenge and rework these early learning experiences if, upon reflection, you see a recurring scenario of little information, pressure, criticism, or fear.

Exercise: Explore Your Sexual Self

This exercise is particularly specific to women but some men may also relate. Many girls grow up to become women who believe it is a losing battle to try to gain sexual pleasure because their anatomy and sexual response patterns are so mysterious and different from men. Research indicates the total prevalence of sexual dysfunction for women, including lack of interest in sex, inability to achieve orgasm, or pain during intercourse, is 43 percent.[1] In particular, younger women who are single and experience greater sexual instability in terms of partners and sexual activity have increased stress around the sex act itself. It is more likely that these women will experience sexual pain and anxiety. A large-scale study examining subjective sexual well-being across cultures demonstrated that women report less sexual satisfaction than men.[2] And many studies show that 10 percent of women have never experienced an orgasm, either with a partner or during masturbation.

With little direct communication and labeling, even by educated and feministic women, it is easy for girls to develop an internalized sense of shame and confusion about their anatomy. Deep within the minds of many women lurks the thought that it is somehow unseemly or bad to physically explore their sexual anatomy. The lack of direct labeling about female anatomy contributes to the vulva region existing as a paradoxical no-touch zone for the woman and, yet, a place where men are permitted entrance. Knowing and accepting your body, your sexual anatomy, and how the two operate together is essential for a fulfilling sex life.

Adopt a mindset of acceptance of your body and calm curiosity about how it works. Read about female sexuality—consider *Sex Matters for Women*, by Foley, Kope, and Sugrue or a similar guide to help you to better understand your sexual

---

1 Laumann, E.O., Paik, A. & Rosen, R.C. (1999). Sexual dysfunction in the United States prevalence and predictors. *Journal of the American Medical Association*, 281, 537–544.

2 Laumann, E.O., Paik, A., Glasser, D.B., Kang, J.H., Wang, T., Levinson, B., Moreira, E.D., Nicolosi, A. & Gingell, C. (2006). A cross-national study of subjective sexual well-being among older women and men: Findings from the global study of sexual attitudes and behaviors. *Archives of Sexual Behavior*, 35, 145–161.

self. Communicate with other women about female sexual response patterns. If you allow your sexual self to remain unexplored, confusion and mystery will impede your enjoyment of sex.

Embrace self-exploration. This will allow you to learn how to *feel sexual*, separate from the desires or judgments of others. If you have difficulty feeling comfortable exploring your own body, ask yourself why? What do you fear? What could be more natural? If you do not take an active interest in understanding your sexual self, how can you expect a partner to find that understanding? By challenging the roadblocks to your sexual fulfillment, you will liberate yourself.

Important Note about Hating on Yourself: A necessary prerequisite for becoming comfortable in your own skin is to no longer hate on yourself by cruelly picking at your physical appearance or obsessively doctoring your looks with products and procedures. If you painfully scrutinize your appearance and work to "fix it," you exist in a vigilant state, fearing a flaw will be exposed, feeling awkward, out of sync, and evaluated; all of these qualities increase your sense of self-consciousness, which is antithetical to pleasurable sex. *Studies show that the more preoccupied you are with your physical appearance, the less likely it is that you enjoy your sexual experiences.* For more on how to feel good enough, consider reading the <u>Building Self-Esteem</u> workbook in this series.

Find Your Sexual Voice

Engaging in unguarded communication with romantic partners or trusted friends with whom you can be open and explorative will help you to make thoughtful decisions regarding your sex life. As you communicate about your sexual dilemmas, questions, and insecurities and hear those of others, you will become more comfortable with your sexual voice.

One fantasy many men and women hold says that when sex is with the right partner, it is an easy passion that naturally evolves into uninhibited comfort and ecstasy. Thus, when a steamy courtship devolves into unfulfilling sex, both partners not only feel disappointment but may believe the match itself is fundamentally wrong. Similarly, many women maintain the erroneous and self-defeating belief that if their sexual partner does not intuitively know how to sexually please, then he must not really be "the one."

It is important to be able to tell your partner what you like, including what you like about him or her, and to be curious about their preferences. The reality is that good sex takes self-knowledge and communication. Couples who openly talk about their sexual preferences, desires, needs, turn-ons, and turn-offs have more fulfilling sex lives.

Across the board, open communication about the sex act itself is associated with increased sexual satisfaction for both men and women. When a relationship is just beginning, it is much harder to engage in open dialogue about sexual preferences because, understandably, there is not as much emotional intimacy present. Feeling comfortable when discussing your sex life with your partner is a good sign that emotional intimacy is present.

As you date and pursue close and intimate relationships, take the plunge; be brave by working to develop an authentic dialogue with your partner about sexual preferences.

STEP 4

Get to Know People

When it comes to getting to know new people and dating, popular long-standing advice suggests that until the fish is on the hook, it's beneficial to adhere to certain firm rules. These dating rules purport to offer a formula for finding commitment and true romantic partnership. Many hope that if they play the game correctly, their prince or princess will be the prize. But because playing a game necessarily translates into masking your authentic self, these rules can't possibly deliver the genuine intimacy true love requires.

If we conceive of intimacy as a series of nesting boxes, the innermost box represents the closeness and acceptance you reserve for yourself. Everything that follows depends on the integrity of that first box. Subsequent boxes represent other people, and these boxes must fit nicely around the first box if there is to be intimacy.

Problem: "Dating doesn't work."
Cure: Cultivate a fresh perspective.

Reconsider your opinions about dating in order to open yourself to the possibilities of a new approach. Put yourself in novel situations, change your mindset, and learn to tolerate rejection in a healthy manner. Taking this new perspective into the dating world will help you have a different kind of experience and perhaps attract a different type of partner.

Put Yourself in New Situations

If you continue to think and do the same things you have always thought and experienced, you will remain stuck. Your brain is more elastic than you might think. It can adapt and grow if you expose it to new experiences. Perhaps there are things that you like or have wanted to try but have been afraid to do. As long as they reflect *your genuine interests*, consider taking up these pursuits immediately.

Consider not only new activities, but new daily routines, routes to work, food choices, and restaurant choices. Work to experience new aspects of your personality or bring back to life old parts of yourself that have gone dormant.

For example, Julie played the guitar as a child and then gave up the instrument as an adult. After her divorce, and at forty years of age, she started lessons and eventually joined a band. This allowed Julie to reconnect with a part of herself that not only brought her joy, but also became a way to be in new situations and around different personalities. For Tiffany, a difficult break up in her early 20s and the resulting heartbreak forced her to dig deep into what was missing from her life. This exploration motivated her to pursue a PhD in art history.

If the idea of new situations, new activities, and new people brings you stress or anxiety, think about the consequences of too much fear of rejection.

Tolerate Rejection

An unexamined fear of rejection has the power to influence every decision you make and can prevent you from getting what you want out of life. This is never more true than for those who have trouble getting close to others. Pursuing the same unsuccessful relationship patterns over and over is a way for people to play it safe and not confront their fear of rejection. If you avoid learning to better manage rejection, you too will deny yourself the relationships you desire.

You should know that most people are rejected and hurt on the way to finding a lasting and healthy commitment. Gear yourself up for this process. Remind yourself that if you are persistent, despite rejection, you will eventually be successful in your quest for closeness and intimacy with a romantic partner.

In Carol Dweck's theory of success, she found that the mindset we hold about our abilities (fixed or growth) impacts the way we process rejection. In one study, people were asked to describe a time in their lives when they were painfully rejected by a significant other. The stories people told were all sad and even heart-breaking, but their mindset determined how effectively people managed their particular situation**s**.

Those who hold a fixed mindset about themselves tend to feel damaged as a result of the rejection, as if they have been deemed ultimately unlovable. Because this judgment is experienced by fixed mindset individuals as *permanent and irreparable*, they have no strategies for managing these awful feelings. Instead of working through their emotions, fixed mindset individuals tend to put their energies into gaining revenge or getting back at the one who wounded them. While growth mindset individuals experienced hurt and sadness, they considered ways in which they would *proceed differently in their next relationship*. Growth mindset individuals focus on forgiveness, letting go, and specific relationship skills they plan to improve upon in the future.[3]

Exercise: Tolerate rejection.
Use the following questions to show yourself you can learn to tolerate rejection.

- Write down the basic details of three occasions from the past that left you feeling unloved, left out, not good enough, or cut off from an individual or group of people that you had been close to.

- What are you saying to yourself about the hurt or what the hurt means about you as a person? Instead of globally writing yourself off—"I suck"—can you come up with a specific relationship skill you could work to improve?

- What are your thoughts about the person or people you feel are rejecting you?

- Are you putting the person/people on a pedestal? Remember, no one is perfect. It is likely they have their own difficulties, just like everyone else.

---

3 Dweck, C.S. (2006). *Mindset: The New Psychology of Success*. Random House: New York.

- Are you angry and holding a grudge? Remember that carrying anger and a grudge only keeps the pain of rejection alive. See if you can let it go, or, if not, start working toward letting it go.

- Does the rejection feel like a permanent stain on your record? If so, can you recognize that the rejection has passed, and that it is only alive in your mind right now? You can start again. You can build new connections.

- Is there anything good that has come or could come from the rejection?

- Is there anything you learned from this relationship that could positively affect your next relationship?

Going forward, give yourself permission to be rejected or to be unwanted from time to time. Show yourself that you are strong enough to tolerate it. Most people feel frustrated with love until it works. Rejection is part of the process of finding the right match, not a statement about your worth as an individual.

Change Your Relationship Mindset

Carol Dweck, in her theory of success, found that the mindset you hold about your abilities (fixed or growth) shapes how successful you may be in developing productive relationships. *A fixed view of relationships means you believe relationships are either meant to be or not meant to be. A growth belief means you believe healthy relationships take time and effort to develop.* Her findings indicate that those who hold fixed beliefs tend to end relationships at the first sign of discontent.[4] Interestingly, those with strong growth beliefs have fewer one-night stands.

Maintaining a mindset with the belief that relationships are either meant to be or not meant to be leads to a fantasy that on a very special day in the future, you will find your Prince Charming, and all will be right in the world. Once Prince Charming inevitably disappoints, you become defeated.

---

4 Dweck, C.S. (2000). *Self-Theories: Their role in motivation, personality, and development.* Psychology Press: New York, London. See study, Knee, C.R. (1998). Implicit theories of relationships: Assessment and prediction of romantic relationship initiation, coping, and longevity. *Journal of Personality and Social Psychology,* 74, 360–370.

Self-Assessment: What is your romantic mindset? Answer these true or false questions to discover your romantic mindset. The more times you answer true, the more likely it is that you have a fixed mindset when it comes to romance and commitment.

- When I meet the one, he or she will sweep me off my feet.

- If we fight, it's not meant to be.

- If it's hard work, then it's not the right match.

- I don't want to have to work at my relationships.

- I don't believe a good relationship should take work.

- I feel relationships should be completely fun and romantic.

- Once messy feelings come up in my relationships, I make my exit.

- I know I'm with the wrong person if we have conflicts.

- When I'm in the right relationship, I'll know, because we will never fight.

- When I'm with the right person, I will always feel happy.

If you are noticing you have a more fixed approach to love and commitment, open yourself up to the idea that relationships are not black and white. Just as you have strengths and weaknesses, so too do relationships. Consider that each new date or new acquaintance represents an opportunity to grow and learn about yourself. Instead of solely searching for "the one," notice how various partners challenge you and use conflict as a way to improve your communication skills. Assess how well your dates communicate and if they make you feel better or worst about conflict. Instead of hoping to be swept off your feet, opt for truly trying to get to know people and seeing if you can fully let them into your world, so they may come to know the real you.

Adopt an outlook that indicates dating will result in meeting the right person and a long-term relationship *eventually*. This will enable you to maintain your self-esteem and more fully appreciate the experience.

Problem: "I HATE going out on dates, I prefer to just 'hang out' with people."
Cure: Get used to the one-on-one.

Texting, hanging out, and hooking up have taken away some pressure, so that many feel more free and at ease when meeting new people. In fact, according to *USA Today*, an online survey found that 69 percent of 2,647 singles ages 18–59 years are "at least somewhat confused" about whether any given outing with a possible romantic partner is or is not a date.

Fears of being vulnerable and awkward in first encounters are minimized by the practices of hooking up and hanging out and the concept of "friends with benefits." By taking away the formalities and the scary word "date," people are free to be more impersonal and they feel less exposed. Hanging out or no-strings-attached hooking up takes the personal onus away. So when a relationship doesn't jell, the outcome is not experienced as a rejection because, after all, how can a person lose if he or she is not playing the game?

At the same time, these relaxed expectations mean certain important romantic skills are underdeveloped. The just-hanging-out attitude means many do not take the relationships that do begin to bud seriously and may be quite uncomfortable when it comes to emotional intimacy.

Facebook and other social media contribute to this attitude by providing a ready medium to gain information without actually having to fully bring one's self to the table. The more a person engages in these arm's-length encounters, the more uncomfortable a real date becomes.

Habitually relying on these practices allows people to hide their innermost selves while still enjoying a superficial level of romantic attention. Yet in order to find a more fulfilling match, it is essential to learn to be at ease in a one-on-one dating context where both parties know that the other is evaluating them as a potential romantic partner.

Why Those Awkward One-on-One Dates Matter

You might ask, "Why?" Being vulnerable—which means not hiding but bringing your full self forward—is a key to forging lasting relationships built on authentic emotional intimacy. Of course, a willingness to be vulnerable builds over time as couples become more and more intimate. But when a person is risking almost zero vulnerability, as is generally the case with hanging out, hooking up, and friends with benefits, the resulting match is based more on fantasy than real life.

Whatever awkward moments take place between a new couple during those first few dates—for example, pregnant pauses over a first meal together, inadvertently cutting each other off while speaking, the forced politeness or the inelegance of planning and executing an outing with a complete stranger: these are the seeds that must be sown to learn if a partnership can grow.

The tension and awkwardness of dealing with new people in a one-on-one context are difficult for many. A new date is a trip into the unknown, neither individual has a sure feel for how the other will behave or respond. As a result, people have to work much harder at first encounters than they do with hook up partners or with people they know very well. Most feel exposed when they have to work with someone unknown.

If you cannot allow some of this vulnerability, you may find yourself continually hooking up and hanging out with the same types, just to avoid the tension of the unknown. Keep in mind, however, that there are no shortcuts to developing real emotional intimacy with a potential romantic partner. Using hooking up or hanging out to circumvent the harder job of a real date means the necessary work you need to do to prepare yourself is only mounting.

Challenge Your Habitual Dating Tendencies (Even If It Feels Weird at First):

- A date is when you personally ask someone out or a person asks you out, to do a specific activity. A one-on-one hangout is often mentioned casually over text or social media, or in an indirect manner, which may cause you to wonder, "Does he or she want to hang out with me, I can't tell." An example of a direct date is "I want to take you out to dinner" or "Would you like to go to this concert with me?" A hang out is "What are you up to tonight" with no direct follow up or plan, and perhaps hours later you get a text: "Come over."

- Dating or direct one-on-one encounters help relationships start on a healthy footing. Stop attempting to skip this step. Instead, push yourself to do it again and again—eventually you will become more comfortable with dating. If you only date a certain kind of person, then you end up with a limited applicant pool.

- Deliberately tell your dates that you are looking for a real relationship. Do not feel embarrassed or ashamed. How can you get what you want if you don't tell yourself and the universe that you want it? If you don't say it, you will attract partners who are grateful you are not expressing this desire, which means they don't really want a real relationship themselves. *All of this would be fine and is fine, unless a relationship with genuine emotional intimacy is what you desire.* Be honest with yourself. Presumably you are reading this book because you want the whole package. If that is the case and you have not admitted it to yourself, do so promptly, so you can get on with it.

- Communicating through text and social media is not sufficient. You need to see the body language and facial expressions of your partners, and they need to see yours in order to stir empathy and a deeper connection. If you overly rely on text and social media, then the mutual affinity you are trying to build may not be authentic. And if you rely on these modes early on in the relationship, then it begins to feel awkward to talk directly or on the phone. Avoid all of this by only using electronic modes to meet new people and/or to set up times and outings for one-on-one interaction. If you start to have a more serious conversation via text, e-mail, or social media, ask if you can talk on the phone or in person. This is a great way to screen out people who are not yet mature enough to have an emotionally connected partnership. There is no substitute for face-to-face meetings and speaking directly on the phone.

- Flashes of discomfort are the cost when a person allows themselves to be a little vulnerable with a stranger. The level of vulnerability involved on a first date is, of course, not as encompassing as the vulnerability a couple willingly opens themselves up to in a longer-term relationship. But, these small moments are an entrée to emotional closeness; they give you a hint of what it will be like to be unguarded with this particular person in the future.

- Men and women both control the date. It is not solely the man's responsibility to do the asking or to find the appropriate venue. And women who ask men out are not weird, aggressive, or cougars. If you find someone interesting, directly ask him or her for a one-on-one outing. Reduce the tension by progressing from a very short date to longer dates. For example, if it is someone new to you, start with coffee, ice cream, and casual conversation. Once you have had a few brief meetings with a particular person who makes you feel good and at ease, then consider increasing the time spent together during your next date.

Problem: "I don't want to seem desperate, so I play hard to get or put on a bit of an act."
Cure: Assess your partners from *your* perspective.

People are often told the following: Don't be the first to call or to say "I love you" or to express any sense of emotional neediness. They are also told that after an interaction, they should wait at least three days to initiate contact. These rules of thumb are about self-protection and not exposing yourself to possible rejection. The problem is that partnership and love are built on a foundation that includes the prospect of vulnerability. If you want to call or text after a pleasant date or meeting with someone new, but you continually stop yourself because it is too soon, you are closing a path to spontaneous intimacy.

Boundaries are important, particularly when you are meeting people for the first time, but if you suppress every urge to reveal your feelings to dates or partners, you will never learn their capacity for emotional intimacy. If someone close to you meets your genuine expression with rejection, teach yourself not to take it personally. This can be hard, particularly for some of us, but try to recognize the primary, inherent value in being yourself. That trumps any gamesmanship from others and helps you figure out where you stand in your relationships.

Women sometimes adopt the "be easy, light and giggly" mindset, not wanting to intimidate dates or come off as too aggressive. This is because in our culture, girls and women are often conditioned to be a bit ditzy, as they learn that this attracts male flirtation. And boys and men still see models of this behavior in popular media. All of this tends to dumb down both sexes. If giggling doesn't match your true mood at a particular moment—or if your genuine personality is much more serious than that—then your date will not be getting to know the true you. If you have to dumb down your personality for companionship, how will you find a true companion for the real you? This behavior also ignores how much men do value real women who can be fully and deeply engaged in their lives. In reality, men report that, over the long term, they want their partners to have their own opinions, lives, and serious thoughts.

Similarly, some men adopt a Mr. Mysterious manner or a noncommittal, aloof front to keep female emotional intimacy needs at bay. Some women may find the mysterious male intoxicating and are energized by the prospect of making him so thoroughly enamored of her that he will reveal his true self. Sadly, this result rarely occurs, as the man in question (for his own reasons) is uncomfortable being fully open to and known by his romantic interests. All the mystery is composed of superficiality, and it brings despair when the relationship never gets out of first gear.

Instead of playing the game, work to be your real self, so you will only attract those who actually like the real you. In addition, rather than spending your time trying to mollify your dates, work to assess what a real relationship with a particular person would be like.

Deliberately Assess Your Dates

If your priority is to be liked and desired by others, then you will blame yourself whenever something goes wrong. Instead of objectively seeing a potential partner as he or she is, you will spend your time focusing on what you can do, or how you can act, to achieve their love.

Consider if focusing too much on your flaws or putting on an act is causing you to neglect the importance of experiencing your partners from your *own perspective*. Instead of fearing rejection, work to assess your potential partners from your point of view.

<u>Self-Assessment: Questions to ask yourself during or after new dates.</u> Reflect on these questions as you date and casually meet new people. Notice if your responses stay skin deep after four or five outings or if they deepen.

- What is the primary feeling when you are around this person? Are you excited, at ease, content, strong, grounded? Are you anxious, guarded, tenuous, or insecure? Now, are these feelings that you always have with new people? Or can you identify something specific about your date and the interaction that is generating the feeling?

- Does this person's influence take you to a better place or a worse place?

- Who are you when you are in the person's presence: are you yourself or are you playing a role?

- Does this person bring out your healthy self or your unhealthy self?

- Is this person similar to your past partners? If so, is he or she similar in good ways or in bad ways?

- Does the person show a genuine interest in wanting to know you on various levels?

- Is the person reliable, that is, does he or she keep dates and commitments with you, show up on time?

- Do you feel calm in the person's presence?

- Does the person seem mysterious and complicated, causing you to feel empty or confused after the interaction?

- Is the person giggly and flirty but without substance?

- Does the person seem better than you—smarter, richer, funnier? Even if this is true, is the person acting like someone on a higher plane or do you feel like his or her equal?

- Do you feel secure that you will hear from this person again or are you on pins and needles about it?

- Do you feel as if you want to be perfect when you are around the person?

- Or do you lose yourself in the conversation?

- Do you feel inadequate during or after the date?

- Or do you feel full and good about yourself during and after the date?

- Do you feel engaged, curious, and open when you're with the person?

- Does the person share things about himself or herself but also ask about you?

- Does the person try to get to know many different parts of you?

- Do you laugh with the person?

- Do you feel as if the person is only connecting with you as a sexual object?

- Do you feel like the person is only thinking about you to determine what you can do for him or her?

- Do you feel comfortable expressing what you like about him or her?

- Does the person openly tell you what is likable about you?

- What do you imagine it would be like to be vulnerable or more open about yourself with this particular person? Do you think he or she would listen and be kind or create distractions to avoid the topic and your feelings?

As you ask yourself these questions, notice the ratio of anxiety and discomfort to calm and contentedness. If the anxiety is frequent and the calm feelings are quite rare, ask yourself if this is the best match for you. If after a few dates you continue to feel more anxious than comfortable, consider that this is a budding relationship that will probably not bring you longer-term happiness.

Problem: "I'm always worried about 'giving the milk away for free.' When is it okay to have sex with a new partner?"
Cure: Cultivate authentic sexual experiences.

Individuals are often advised to experience a specific number of dates before having sex. There is a flaw in this approach. People don't necessarily achieve emotional intimacy after two, three, or four dates. No arbitrary amount of time corresponds to what truly helps to build enjoyable sexual experiences for men and women.

In order for sex to be enjoyable and safe, most people need to feel a modicum of trust and emotional intimacy. For some, this happens in a short period of time; for others, trust takes much longer to develop. Judge each date or new partner as a unique individual.

Consider adopting the following policy when it comes to sex with new partners:

- Instead of operating against a three-date deadline, notice how you feel when you're in this person's presence. This is a good indication of how the sexual experience will be. Is he/she interested in knowing you on more than one level? Does he/she ask questions about you and listen to your responses? Can you talk openly about what it would be like to have a sexual relationship, or does this cause tremendous anxiety and awkwardness?
- Each time you engage in sex for impulsive reasons, including to gain attention, a self-esteem boost, an immediate physical release, or to briefly escape being alone, you reinforce a pattern of not allowing others in on a deeper, more meaningful level. Notice if you are reducing someone to a sexual object and force yourself to slow down and enjoy other things about them that you find attractive: personality, sense of humor, work, hobbies, or just being fun to talk to and spend time with.
- Notice when you disconnect from a sexual experience due to obsessive focus on your partner's comfort or pleasure, worrying about what he or she may be thinking about you, or what their sexual experience of you might be. Instead, pay attention to how this thinking spiral is inhibiting

47

you. Redirect your attention toward your own pleasure, as well as your physical and mental sensations.

- Consider not proceeding with a sexual encounter unless you have compelling evidence from your experience with the person, through open communication and emotional intimacy, that pleasure will ensue. If you go forward with a sexual experience and then become aware that you are zoning or numbing out, consider stopping the sexual encounter. If you go forward with a particular partner and the sex becomes physically painful, by all means stop the encounter.

Problem: "I'm afraid I will mention my ex or otherwise 'let my crazy out.'"
Cure: Maintain boundaries while being real.

On the one hand, yes, you don't want your ex-boyfriend or ex-wife to be the main topic of conversation when meeting someone new. On the other hand, if you are coming out of a marriage or a long-term relationship, it is almost impossible to avoid mentioning this and to also be your true self. It is okay to say what is really going on in your life—just make sure to own your experience of the demise of the relationship, as opposed to endlessly criticizing or name-calling your ex.

In addition, many I talk to are terrified of a new love interest discovering they have "issues." They vow not to mention anything about their dysfunctional family, psychiatric medications, or mood swings to their new dates. The reality is that if you are unstable emotionally—suffering from acute depression, serious mood swings, or debilitating anxiety/panic attacks—now may not be a good time for you to date. You will know you are ready when you feel you can be open about what you are experiencing in a thoughtful manner—using statements such as "I struggle with depression, but I have found therapy helpful" or "I have had to deal with anxiety and now I am at a much better place." In the end, you are going to want a partner who understands emotional issues and who is not going to mark you off his/her list because you are getting help or struggling with a life event.

It is important to have boundaries and to not reveal more or do more than you are completely comfortable with. With that in mind, opening up and getting to know someone does take a certain amount of patience and vulnerability. Assess each new partner as an individual, and stay keenly connected with the way you experience yourself while in his or her presence. If you have a tendency to say too much, then tell your dates this fact about yourself and how you are working to take more time getting to know people. On the other hand, if you are typically reserved or overly guarded, tell your dates you are working to be more open.

You need someone with whom you can reveal your authentic self, not just a piece of you—and you are the only one who can bring that fully forward.

Actively Manage the Relationship

Popular culture embraces romantic notions about love striking when least expected, as if it were something outside of human control, like a lightning storm or an earthquake. One minute a person faces a lonely life without a romantic partner, and in the next, he or she is joyously propelled into the welcoming arms of another person, their course forever changed for the better.

Of course, real life rarely lives up to this fantasy. Conflict is inevitable because you and your partner, or future partner, are two separate beings. Many people imagine what their partner may be thinking or imagine their partner feels certain ways about them (both good and bad), but they may never actually ask or directly say their own thoughts and feelings. You cannot intuit everything about your partner, nor can your partner do the same of you—and this is where the work comes in.

The work of a relationship should be neither arduous or excruciatingly painful. But do give up the idea that the passion and romance of new love will take care of all the messy details. The work in a romantic relationship is akin to developing an emotionally connected platonic friendship.

Some believe they cannot have it all—you cannot have passion and lust and an emotionally intimate relationship with the same partner. Dividing potential partners according to romance or friendship is a set-up for failure. You must build a working friendship with your partner, one where you can be open and where you have readily available ways to both connect and to resolve conflict.

The tools in this chapter are designed to help you cultivate emotional intimacy with the person you have chosen as your romantic partner. First and foremost, you need to notice if you and your partner are both working for the relationship to progress.

Problem: "How do I know this will be for the long-term?"
Cure: Your relationship should be progressing.

There is perhaps nothing more exciting than new love. The mind darts about, imagining future dates, traveling, meeting one another's friends and families, and one day maybe even marriage or a family. But wait: There is always the possibility that it won't work out. That something terrible will go wrong. That your judgment is off and your new partner is not the person you thought he or she was. How do you protect yourself amid all this excitement and vulnerability?

Believe in The Honeymoon Period

The relationship will not progress if it is toxic from the start. Like a bruised apple, a relationship that begins with disrespect, unkindness, or emotional avoidance is only going to become more unpleasant. You should feel generally at ease early on. If you are always on the spot, anxious, wondering, worrying, and ruminating, take this as information that reveals how this person is impacting you. Ignoring this important information about how you feel in the presence of a new love interest sets you up for trouble in the long term. Some relationships endure for painful years even though the negative signs were on full display at the beginning.

Finding love is wonderful, but it's important not to be swept away, passively entering relationships that hold little prospect of ever meeting your emotional needs.

Take the case of Eliza. She comes to therapy troubled over the end of her three-year relationship with Sam. As she talks about the events that transpired when she first met Sam, she paints a picture of a difficult courtship; for the first eleven months, she never felt as if she was in a "real" relationship. Sam was unwilling to fully commit. They never met one another's families. Their courtship was mostly after dark. They rarely went on one-on-one outings or dates together. This was immensely frustrating to Eliza at the time, but she found comfort by telling herself that Sam had "a lot of baggage," and that it was in her best interest to not push too hard to progress beyond the hanging out mode.

Around the one-year mark, something changed. Sam managed to be somewhat more open in his affection for Eliza, and he began dating her in a direct manner. In their second year together, he introduced her to his family. Eliza felt as though all of her hard work had finally paid off—in a way, that made landing Sam feel even more special. She saw it, briefly, as an achievement—briefly because these were only temporary improvements. As time wore on, she saw that the issues present from day one were never fully overcome. She was always the one steering the ship—drawing him out of his shell, initiating plans and difficult conversations, working to get to know his family, and making every effort possible to keep Sam connected to her.

Couples who have happy, committed relationships for the long term typically have emotional intimacy present early on. This means your partner may not be able to say, "You're the one, let's get married next week," but he or she should be able to say, "I am really enjoying getting to know you and can see us being very happy together." As the relationship progresses over time, emotional intimacy should also gradually progress. Talking about what you each want in the future should become easier, and more specific.

If you are the only one working to advance the relationship, you and it will burn out. Notice if your relationship remains stuck in first gear. If it is stuck, something's wrong.

How You Can Help Your Relationship to Progress

Here are a few specific skills that, if implemented by both you and your partner, will help your relationship to move forward in a healthy manner. Mastering these skills now will make the hard knocks of relationship life much easier to manage later on.

Routines of Separate and Together Time: People cope with the vulnerability that comes when falling in love in one of two ways—they either hold too tightly or they hold too loosely. If you hold too tightly, then you may engulf the other person and be perceived as overly demanding. You may have expectations for constant togetherness time or a rigid commitment that the relationship is just not yet sturdy enough to handle. When your partner leaves, you may find yourself ill at ease, unsure of what to do with yourself when not in their presence. Alternatively, if you hold too loosely, you may become avoidant when your new love talks of their emotions or their needs. You may make yourself inconsistently available to your partner. Your partners may attempt to chase you down or try to elicit commitments from you that you are unable to directly address. The key is balance. Expect too much too soon, and the cart will go before the horse and topple over. But, if you are separate too much, then the relationship doesn't have the petri dish of mutual experiences it needs to grow and flourish. Relationships need time together and apart to become safe and comfortable. It is a balance that takes some deliberate thought.

Routines of Relating: Typically, couples develop weekly rituals over the first few months of dating. Rituals could be such activities as watching a certain show every week, breakfast on Saturdays, cooking a meal together, or a weekly sporting event. The point is it should be a regular routine that you both look forward to and something you are both committed to. Even if you miss a week, you automatically pick it back up the next. These routines of relating will expand and change over time, but some simple activities to connect on a regular basis should be present early on.

Routines of Disclosure: Understanding your partner's family, past experiences, deeper motivations, more complicated emotions, as well as revealing yours, is a process that occurs gradually over time. But it starts early on. If you and your partner are falling in love, then it's natural to be curious and to ask questions about one another. Work to be open while keeping boundaries. Only say what you feel safe revealing. Allow time between revelations so as to not overwhelm your partner. Too much, too quick turns a romance into constant therapy. You want to be having fun together, but also to reveal yourselves to each other over time.

Routines of Decision Making: One pattern that may lead to a lingering half-love that never gets off the ground comes when a couple progresses in the external aspects of their life together but not in terms of their emotional understanding of one another. If you meet his family because you happened to run into them, move in together because your lease ran out and you needed a place to stay, become dog owners because a friend was moving abroad and needed someone to take her pet, etc., etc., you never have the opportunity to talk through decisions as a couple. When decisions are not directly made together, it becomes easy for one member of the union to not take the commitment seriously—after all, it occurred by happenstance, as in "I never said I wanted you to move in; you needed a place to stay." Making conscious decisions together helps to cement commitment and also enables couples to discover more about one another and what each person wants for the long-term.

Routines of Accountability: Own it when you make a mistake, let your partner down, hurt his or her feelings, or fail to follow through on what you said you were going to do. Tell your partner directly. Even if you find yourself at some point no longer committed to the relationship, don't just passively let it dissolve. Expect the same from your partner. If a person says he or she will show up at seven and doesn't arrive until eight, they should notice this and be able to explain the situation to you. If the date acts like "It's no big deal" or doesn't even bring it up at all, you should be curious about whether that person can hold himself or herself accountable. Relationships inevitably have conflict, but if both you and your partner can hold yourselves accountable right from the start, this will massively impact your ability to more easily glide through disagreement. Trust and safety grow when people can genuinely say, "My bad, I'm sorry."

A general sense of ease should be present early on, and this ease should only increase in depth and intensity over time. If this feeling is not progressing, there is a chance the union may never get off the ground. If you are in a relationship that is progressing, be grateful and allow yourself to enjoy it. It can be tempting to immediately push for more. Instead, allow yourself to be fully present as you enjoy the moment of falling in love. You can never get this time back.

Problem: "Sometimes I think I'm in a really unhealthy relationship, and then other times it feels terrific."
Cure: Assess the patterns in the relationship.

You may be saying to yourself or others, "This HAS to work...I have already introduced her to my family and spent a year getting to know her" or "How will I ever find another boyfriend/girlfriend?" or "I am getting old...my childbearing years are passing me by."

This mindset makes it difficult to accurately assess if your partner is the right long-term match for you. Instead of coming to grips with what may be immutable flaws, you make excuses or rationalizations to justify the union. Also, appreciate the pressure you are putting on yourself by not accepting the possibility that this relationship does not have to result in marriage.

You can always exit, even if it brings you fear and sadness. These feelings will eventually pass. Instead of worrying, spend your time getting to know him or her, observing how you feel in that person's company and how he or she responds to what you reveal about yourself. Be brave, so you can actually figure out who this person is.

Assess the Emotional Health Of Your Partner

The emotional health of your partner is also a potential stumbling block. You have baggage that you are likely sorting through, and your partner will have baggage too. You need to be fully aware of what kind of issues your partner or potential partner is bringing into your life. Issues may not necessarily be toxic if both members of the relationship are aware and can make meaningful effort toward growth. But, you must be clear-eyed in making the determination.

Certain personality types generally, that is, most of the time, lead to unhappiness and frustration in relationships. Assess if your partner falls into any of the personality categories below. If your partner tends to chronically and pervasively engage you and the world from one of the frameworks below, consider that you may need to withdraw. Isolated incidents don't count as pervasive patterns.

The Narcissist: Narcissists have a deep need to be admired and valued. As a result, they present a false self, one that appears superior, above others, ultra-confident. This façade masks a fragile self that cannot take in the slightest bit of criticism or take responsibility for how they impact others. During the early stages of dating, the narcissist may come across as charming, alluring you with flattery, adoration, and romantic outings. Once the narcissist feels he or she has you, the romance wanes. You may start to have the sense that the person is always on the lookout for something better. The relationship feels tenuous, not safe, not secure. When you are together, the narcissist talks about himself or herself incessantly or tunes you out and cannot offer you (or others) true empathy. Even if you are struggling with something serious, inevitably, the energy turns back to the person's needs, or he or she seems to not really take in what you are communicating. The narcissist operates solely based on what works best for them, failing to follow through on commitments with you unless it perfectly suits them in that moment. And, the narcissist expects you to give him or her what they want immediately or angrier, even irate behavior, may result.

The Passive Aggressive: People who are chronically passive aggressive have extreme difficulty being direct with the people in their lives about what they need and feel. They often grow up in environments where they were powerless to get their needs met and where they did not have a voice. As a result, passive aggressive people express difficult emotions or complicated needs indirectly—sarcasm, silent treatment, joking. Passive aggressive people often say one thing but do another—

"Yes, I can't wait to meet your mom"—but then when you suggest specific times to meet her, they will not commit and are vague about why. When you point out that their behavior doesn't match what they are telling you, they often present themselves as victims and turn the tables on you—calling out your flaws and inadequacies—or use distraction to not confront the issue. As an example, every time Tom brought up a future with his girlfriend Lisa, she would immediately change the topic. He finally confronted her on this, and she offered Tom superficial flattery, but she still could not talk about the deeper aspects of the commitment. The problem for Tom was that Lisa never directly said, "I don't want a future with you" or "I don't see this going anywhere," and so he was left to wonder, guess, doubt himself, and ultimately try harder. Notice if your partner is not being direct with you. Expect that he or she will and should talk of the future without extreme awkwardness. If your partner is not able to do that, there may be more going on than he or she can allow themselves to say directly to you.

The Emotionally Unavailable: The emotionally unavailable partner is not always as easy to spot. This person often initially acts attentive and interested in long-term commitment. But then, suddenly and surprisingly, the person makes you feel as if you are simply an acquaintance. Emotionally unavailable people work to manage relationships so they don't have to experience any kind of vulnerability in the union. For example, Emma would enjoy a great weekend with her boyfriend. Then, when Sunday morning rolled around, she felt abruptly kicked out of his apartment. He would give no explanation about his plans for the day or why she needed to leave, but would suddenly make things very awkward for her. In that moment, Emma felt that her partner saw her as a casual acquaintance.

Just as you get close and feel as if you are getting closer, notice if your partner directly or indirectly pulls back.

To take another example, Madison and her boyfriend regularly spent Friday nights together. However, out of nowhere, he might pull out of the usual plan with a message that said, "I can't make it tonight, enjoy your evening." Then, just as Madison began to accept that he was not where she was emotionally, he would suddenly want to get close again.

The dominant emotion with an emotionally unavailable partner is confusion about what's going on and/or the status of the relationship. You doubt yourself, and this person feeds off this because you keep giving him/her the benefit of the doubt. You would rather be wrong and wanted by your partner than right, in which case you would have to let him or her go. If your partner fits this description, accept that he or she is not emotionally available, let go of this relationship, and you will save yourself a lot of frustration.

The Addict: If your partner becomes intoxicated or drinks a great deal of alcohol each time you hang out together, or has a drug or pornography addiction, take this data very seriously. Addicts who have not confronted the illness and who have not yet received adequate treatment are typically in denial. If you bring up the addict's tendencies, he or she is probably going to try to talk you out of your conclusion. Trust your gut. It matters if, more times than not, he or she is in an altered state or vague and evasive about his or her behavior. If the person has no awareness and no desire to receive treatment or otherwise work on the addiction, consider this a deal breaker. Otherwise, you are signing on to be your partner's enabler—not lover.

Self-Assessment: Observe the patterns of the relationship.
Generally, the patterns of a relationship are set early on and have the potential to dominate throughout a couple's years together. Reflect on the relationship balance, in terms of the sexual and emotional patterns you notice in your relationship, to determine if this is the right match for the long term. These assessments are to be completed, not after a new date, but once you have had a number of interactions with a particular partner or feel as if you are in a relationship. Revisit over time as you know one another better.

Relationship Balance Assessment:

- Are you always the one doing the work?
- Is your partner asking more of you than you can give?
- Do you initiate all of the dates and outings?
- Are you invariably the one to bring up difficult discussions or topics?

- Do you frequently need time away from your partner?
- Do you feel you would see your partner much less frequently if you did not initiate interactions?
- Do you see your friends and family members as well as your partner's friends and family, or are you mostly living in your partner's world?
- Do you avoid your partner or feel your partner avoids you for long periods of time?
- Do you feel if you stopped working for the relationship, it would fizzle out?
- Do you want to see your partner all of the time and put pressure on them to see you more?

Notice if you feel overly needy or are overly accommodating to your partner. If so, hold back and see if your partner will pick up the slack. Work on enjoying and staying connected to other aspects of your life beyond just this relationship. Remember: relationships need together and alone time to grow in a healthy way. Try to talk to your partner about what you are observing and working on. If they don't get it or take more initiative, the union may not be a balanced one.

Sexual Assessment:

- Do you feel inhibited or overly concerned about your appearance when in the presence of your partner?
- Do you feel your partner values you, but only when it is convenient to do so or only in a sexual context?
- Do you feel that if you gain weight, your partner will stop desiring you?
- Do you fantasize about doing other nonsexual activities with your partner but, in actuality, spend little time together outside of a sexual context?
- Are you hoping that sex will eventually elicit a commitment from your partner or pull them closer to you?
- Do you let go sexually and feel open to new experiences with your partner?
- Do you enjoy the sexual experiences you have had together?
- Can you talk about your sex life with your partner without extreme awkwardness?

Notice if your relationship is developing in a balanced, sexually and emotionally intimate manner. As your sexual relationship evolves, your partner's genuine curiosity and interest in knowing you should also increase.

Emotional Intimacy Assessment:

- What is the dominant emotion in the relationship? Do you generally feel at ease, calm, happy, or do you feel anxious, fearful?
- Does the relationship make you happy but also feel fragile?
- Are certain topics are off limits with your partner?
- Are you careful and excessively thoughtful about his/her reactions before you bring up certain issues or topics?
- Are you more likely to talk with your friends about your upsets than with your partner?
- Are you afraid or anxious about asking your partner what their level of commitment is in the relationship?
- When you are upset can you talk to your partner about your feelings and does it bring relief or comfort?
- Do you feel you could share almost anything with your partner and you would still receive love or respect?
- Is your partner open with you, in his or her own way, about personality, needs, and struggles?

Emotional intimacy is likely the most important ingredient in long-term fulfillment. In fact, after using data from a study of human development spanning many years—the Grant Study—Harvard researcher Robert Waldinger found that the happiest and physically healthiest people in old age are those who maintain close and intimate relationships. A relationship is not close if you cannot bring your emotions to the table and feel relief and comfort through your partner and if your partner cannot do the same with you. Becoming emotionally close to your partner is not immediate, but safety and connection should exist from the get-go and only increase over time. You want to ultimately feel you can discuss anything, albeit respectfully, and still love and be loved by your partner. Assess this factor very carefully. Without emotional intimacy, there is little comfort in marriage or in a long-term commitment.

Problem: "I want more closeness with my partner or future partner."
Cure: Work on your communication skills.

An effective way to obtain an all-around healthier relationship—including closeness, emotional intimacy, better sex and the ability to more easily resolve conflict—will come to you if you strengthen your communication skills. You cannot necessarily improve the communication skills of your partner or future partner. But research suggests people are attracted to people who have similar communication abilities. So, take this opportunity now to start working on how you communicate. This will positively impact your current and future relationships.

Talk to Your Partners about Your Relationship

Many cherish the fantasy that, once present, true love just takes over and happens. And in that happy state, awkward conversations about what you both want from a long-term relationship are not necessary. The magic of destiny handles the details. It is often those who crave to be loved and cared for the most who find themselves passively wishing and waiting—not directly communicating. They do not take the initiative because they are afraid of what they may hear from their partner. Those caught in this mindset spend too much of their time pulling petals from flowers—"He loves me, He loves me not." Passively obsessing about the future means missing valuable opportunities to better learn who your partner is in the present.

Make it a habit, even early on, to become comfortable talking with your partner about your relationship. Whether what you are experiencing is good or bad, it is important to have meta-conversations around how things are going and how you are both feeling.

For example, if you notice a troubling pattern involving you, or your partner, or both of you, talk about it. This is when we learn the most about the health of our relationships and their potential for growth. Can you get somewhere with the issues you are noticing, and can you hear out your partner on what he or she is experiencing?

If you tell your partner that you really like him and you want to improve the relationship, and he looks away, changes topics, jokes with you, or teases you, he is letting you know that he is unable or unwilling to reciprocate your level of intimacy. If this pattern continues, accept that your partner is not giving you what you want and move on.

ACTIVELY MANAGE THE RELATIONSHIP

If you are feeling confused in your relationship or getting mixed signals from your partner, talk to him or her about it in detail. Perhaps she is afraid or overwhelmed by the future. If she can talk about this in an open and straightforward way, you have made progress toward emotional intimacy and toward being known to one another—important ingredients for long-term love.

Just as important as discussion of the difficult aspects of your relationship is regular communication with your partner about what you appreciate in him or her. Communicate fondness and admiration, and expect this in return. Building healthy habits where you both talk about the good in one another and in the relationship will increase the overall self-esteem of the relationship.

Be honest with yourself about what it is you really want. Make a pact with yourself to directly talk about your wishes. As you become open about what you want, your relationship will grow in ways that you may have not yet experienced. Or you will learn that a partner is not able to give what you desire, in which case you may need to end the relationship. It is a risk to be open, but one worth taking for your emotional well-being.

Just Say It

I'm often saddened when I hear how many years a couple has suffered when one partner wonders about the answer to a question that only the other partner can answer. The partners live trapped between being deeply desirous of relief and being terrified of hearing something they cannot imagine bearing. This trapped state maintains the status quo but makes it impossible for either partner to get more out of the union.

For example: John was disappointed, even angry, when his wife stopped having sex with him. He was confused, but he never allowed himself to ask her why. He never asked the question because he was afraid the answer would open the door for her to completely reject him. So a dry spell turned into twenty years of a sexless marriage.

I observed that some couples have conversations with these lines:

"Hey, are you up for it tonight?"
"No, I'm so tired. Maybe tomorrow?"
"You haven't been up for it lately, is everything okay with us?"

John was shocked that people actually spoke so openly to one another about their sex lives.

In different case, a wife in couples therapy confessed that she thought her husband never really wanted to marry her but felt obligated due to her financial circumstances at the time. He was visibly horrified, tearing up, "No, no, not at all, I deeply, deeply wanted to marry you." Holding that question in for 25 years took a toll, but knowing the answer set them free from repetitive arguments that never really got at the heart of the matter.

Find a way to be respectful and kind while you work to say to your partner whatever is on your mind, and create a safe space in which your partner can also share thoughts and feelings without having to fear your overly intense negative reactions or rejection of them.

Here are a few strategies for sharing more of yourself verbally with your partner:

- *Recognize your own experiences with your partner.* Label your emotions out loud when you feel sad, disappointed, or angry. Do not dismiss them. Find the words to describe what you are feeling. And then, consider the reaction you get. Is she receptive? Is she open to your description of the experience, even if she doesn't agree with it? Does he make you feel better when you are upset, or does he judge you and make you feel worse about your emotional self? Couples with emotional intimacy generally feel better after expressing their emotions to each other. Even if they do not agree, there is a sense of comfort and validation.
- *Willingness to directly communicate your thoughts, needs, and desires is essential.* If you never say what you are thinking, how will you know if your partner can give you what you need? Likewise, how can the people in your life get to know the *real* you if you don't share your innermost thoughts? Work to directly express yourself. If you want to spend more time with your partner, say it. Don't manage your feelings indirectly by attempting to make your partner jealous by flirting with others or by angrily attacking him or her. It is a good sign if your partner is willing to hear you out, express a point of view, and negotiate. If your partner laughs you off, makes a joke, starts roughhousing, or causes you to feel embarrassed for talking in such an intimate manner, he or she may not be the match you deserve.

- *Of course people change their minds.* You and your partner may be truly committed to one another and then your feelings change. This is human. What is important is to check in with each other periodically about where you are and make room for the idea that feelings may change. Working from the same page in a relationship helps people to be content, spontaneous, and emotionally safe with their romantic partners. However, the only way to stay on the same page is to talk directly about where you both are and what you both need in the relationship.

Managing Conflict

Conflict is unavoidable in long-term unions. The crucial part is to hear your partner, to feel heard yourself, and to validate one another emotionally. Even if the initial upset is very intense, couples that come back to the conflict later and resolve it do better for the long term. By *resolve*, I don't mean one person is always right and the other person is always wrong, I mean you work to make each other feel better, rather than worse, about the upset.

You have to tolerate the negative emotions of your partner, or that person will come to resent you and walk on eggshells in your presence. Work to hear your partner's complaints and negative emotions, particularly when they are about you. See if you can recognize as true anything being communicated or at least validate the feelings being expressed.

How can you better handle conflict? John Gottman, in his extensive research on divorce and happy marriages, found that not everything about conflict is bad for a marriage. In fact, he found four factors to be specifically destructive to relationships. He called these the *Four Horsemen of the Apocalypse*[5]:

Criticism: Making global attacks on your partner's personality or character—"You are a loser," "You never do x," "You always make me feel x." Instead of global judgments, make a specific complaint in the context of generally liking and caring about your partner: "Next time your mom says she's coming over, I need you to ask me before you agree."

Defensiveness: The result of criticism is often defensiveness. This may take the form of blaming your partner or in some way turning yourself into the victim.

---

5 Gottman, J.M. (1999). *The Seven Principles for Making Marriage Work.* Three Rivers Press: New York, New York.

The best way to avoid chronic defensiveness is to simply try to hear your partner's complaints and take some responsibility for the points raised.

Contempt: Putting oneself on a higher plane than your partner, or communicating your higher status nonverbally through eye rolling, or communicating disgust with your facial expressions. Avoiding contempt means making the relationship a sacred space where neither you nor your partner makes the other feel utterly unlovable or unwanted. Make that a boundary that neither of you crosses.

Stonewalling. This is when one member of the union shuts down, avoids, or stops attending to the conversation. The stonewaller's partner, typically the female, interprets this shutdown as a sign that her counterpart doesn't care about what she is trying to communicate and therefore doesn't care about her. However, in most cases, the stonewaller is actually emotionally overwhelmed or flooded. Shutting down becomes a way to cope and to self-soothe. The opposite member of the union keeps trying to talk, and the stonewaller keeps shutting down, forming a toxic cycle. The key is to notice when your partner shuts down and to agree together that it is okay to take a break and revisit the topic again later.

You don't have to be perfect in a relationship. But work hard, very hard, to avoid the four horsemen outlined above—both in yourself and in the person you choose to be a partner.

Arguments are inevitable. As you talk through your conflicts, adopt a collaborative framework in which you are able to consider your partner's point of view without letting it override your perspective. Work toward a reciprocal communication pattern, where you listen, thoughtfully consider your partner's perspective, and then reconjure your own perspective and voice any discrepancies. This back-and-forth communication occurs over a number of cycles until the matter at hand eventually resolves. In this process, being right is less important than finding a mutually acceptable conflict recovery path. When a relationship is healthy, couples are able to resolve differences in such a way that both members feel better.

Final Note:

Intimacy is a process of being together while at the same time being content within yourself and with your other life pursuits. True closeness with another living being is characterized by the feeling that there is nowhere else you would rather be. This feeling is not bequeathed; rather, it is achieved by individual effort and insight.

Summary of the Five Steps

Step	Action to Take
#1. Get to know yourself.	Depend on yourself (not others) for the heavy lifting of life. Meditate ten minutes each day. Build in healthy routines of functioning (errands, housekeeping, paying bills, exercise and nutrition). Utilize the Feelings Table and Emotional Spreadsheet to start understanding your emotions.
#2. Stop faking it.	Get in touch with the real you and what you fear others will see if you are yourself with them. Beware of cognitive dissonance—don't agree to activities that do not accurately reflect your identity/preferences. Practice recognizing what you like and don't like, and communicate these preferences to others.
#3. Explore your sexual self.	Explore your sexual narrative, experiences, and history with sex as well as your sexual self. Make a space in your life to do this work; stop expecting sex to come easily without knowing yourself on this level.
#4. Get to know people.	Adopt a fresh new perspective on dating that includes a growth mindset (learning from relationships that don't work out), accepting that rejection is a part of the dating process (not a statement of your worth or capacity to find love), and agreeing only to actual real dates as opposed to hanging out.
#5. Actively manage the relationship.	Assess your relationship, and work for it to progress. If you determine it's not progressing, consider ending the union. Build awareness of fantasy versus what is really occurring in the relationship, including its sexual and emotional components. Review communication and conflict resolution skills, and actively practice them.

What Is the Relationship Formula?

*G*etting Close to Others is part of the Relationship Formula Workbook Series, which consists of four brief workbooks designed to help people who struggle with relationships. Whether you are married, single, divorced, new to dating, gay, or straight, this workbook series will increase your relationship preparedness so that you may better find healthy, meaningful partnerships.

As a psychologist, I see people who talk about feeling they are "emotionally flawed" and "incapable of finding healthy love" or who describe a history of dating "losers" or a series of chronically disappointing relationships. They say they have "repetitive relationship issues" and fear they will never crack the code for love and romance, telling me they "have never had a *real* relationship" or beating themselves up with statements like "What is wrong with me, that I can't get what seems so easy for everyone else?"

If you can't get relationships right, constantly feel as if something is wrong with you when it comes to romance, or find you are continually drawn to the same types of disappointing or dysfunctional partners, or all three of these things, then the Relationship Formula Workbook Series offers a way to gain control. Before you pick your next romantic partner, give yourself an opportunity to be all you can be—because that process will help you find all you deserve.

People who struggle with feeling good enough to get what they want out of life, or those who have a history of unfulfilling relationships, typically benefit

GETTING CLOSE TO OTHERS 5 STEPS

from learning new skills. These four workbooks cover managing four key areas of growth:

1. *Breaking Up and Divorce 5 Steps: How to Heal and Be Comfortable Alone*
2. *Building Self-Esteem 5 Steps: How to Feel "Good Enough" about Yourself*
3. *Toxic Love 5 Steps: How to Identify Toxic-Love Patterns and Find Fulfilling Attachments*
4. *Getting Close to Others 5 Steps: How to Develop Intimate Relationships and Still Be True to Yourself*

Many who struggle with relationships alternate between self-blame for not "getting it right" or inflating and romanticizing what they think others have that they cannot get. The statistics on marital abuse, distress, and infidelity paint a different picture. Many marriages are based on unhealthy relationship patterns of codependency, avoidance, living entirely separate lives, and in some cases, emotional abuse. Half of marriages result in divorce, and more than half of second marriages result in divorce. Even couples that stay together for a lifetime are not necessarily happy or healthy. The reality is relationships take work, and even people who are married or appear to have it all have not always done the necessary work.

The Relationship Formula is not about telling you whom to date; rather, it focuses on the one part of romance that you can control—yourself.

The impact relationships, particularly romantic ones, have on our lives cannot be overstated. They influence physical health, psychological well-being, professional success, lifespan, pleasure, and the emotional success of our children or future children. When you decide that working on yourself is a priority, you are taking a step that will powerfully influence the trajectory of most aspects of your life. This change has the potential to ripple out to every relationship—close friendships, parents, siblings, nieces, nephews, work colleagues, and classmates, as well as children born and unborn. By building yourself up, you acquire the capacity to build others up.

Relationships have the power to heal, to connect, and to provide immeasurable warmth to buffer life's harshest realities. On the flip side, destructive relationships are also powerful and can do crushing harm. You have the ability to choose which path you take. If you decide to take this one—that is, building yourself up from the inside out—you must work on believing with every fiber of your being that if you persevere, life will get better.

The Relationship Formula Workbook series is designed to be used on your own or together with a therapist. Oftentimes, working with a therapist can be tremendously effective to help you understand yourself and build more positive patterns of interaction. For other people, going to therapy requires more expense or time than they have. Some simply prefer to do this work on their own. Whichever approach you take is okay, provided persistence rules.

This program is modular, with four separate workbooks. Some may wish to go through all four. Others will prefer to tailor their approach to their specific histories and issues. It is absolutely fine to complete one workbook or to go forth and complete all four. As you read through the steps, you may come up with your own strategies or find idiosyncratic ways to combine the various tools to suit your personality or personal struggle. Keep a notebook of your work so you can review what you have written down and have learned about yourself as you grow through this program. The more you review the material, the more the tools described will become automatic.

The work may seem daunting at first, but what is far harder is a lifetime of frustrating and disappointing attempts at securing love. Just like beginning a new physical exercise program, this work is difficult initially, but with time, the routine becomes easier and easier. You will notice progress, begin to feel better, and have more positive interactions with others. These rewards will reinforce you and, day by day, you will grow.

Made in the USA
Lexington, KY
31 October 2017